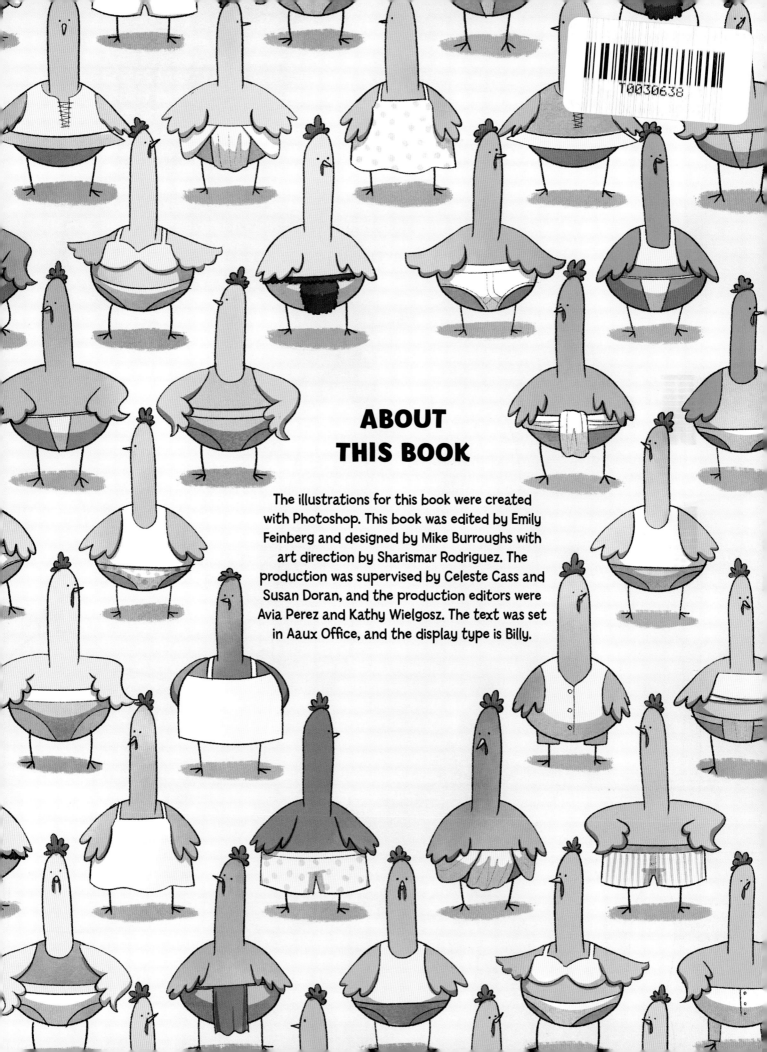

ABOUT
THIS BOOK

The illustrations for this book were created with Photoshop. This book was edited by Emily Feinberg and designed by Mike Burroughs with art direction by Sharismar Rodriguez. The production was supervised by Celeste Cass and Susan Doran, and the production editors were Avia Perez and Kathy Wielgosz. The text was set in Aaux Office, and the display type is Billy.

Roaring Brook Press • New York

A History of Underwear

with PROFESSOR CHICKEN

written by
Hannah Holt

illustrated by
Korwin Briggs

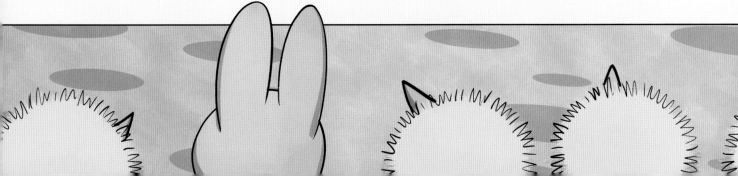

Underwear can be small.

Or big.

Or **HUGE!**

LOCATION:
Austrian Alps

ERA:
3300 BCE

Over five thousand years ago in the Swiss Alps, a hiker named Ötzi became trapped inside a glacier.

Poor Ötzi died, but the ice saved his underwear—a leather
loincloth tied with a belt.

Like Ötzi's underwear, many early
bottom coverings came in pieces.
That's why today we still call them
"a pair."

In fact, easy step-and-go underwear didn't exist back then.
Early hunters and gatherers had to catch their underwear.

Once collected, these animal
hides had to be dried,

pounded,

and smoked.

It took several weeks to produce one sweaty pair of underwear.

Phew. That stinks.

Maybe that's why Egyptians around 1400 BCE preferred linen.

Light and breezy, linen underwear was worn by rich and poor alike in ancient Egypt. Of course, the super rich, like King Tut, wore linen with only the tightest weave and smoothest feel.

Ahh, underwear fit for a king.

Underwear could also be seen as a pile of wealth. How so?
In ancient Egypt, cloth was valuable.
Consider this: Linen starts as flax seeds.
The flax needs to grow.

After it's harvested, it needs to be beaten
and woven into cloth.

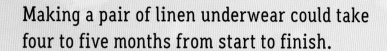

Making a pair of linen underwear could take
four to five months from start to finish.

I need a nap just
thinking about all
that work.

Wearing it was no simple matter either. In the ages before elastic, linen loincloths had to be carefully tied and tucked. One lazy knot and it could roll loose in the middle of the day!

How embarrassing.

LOCATION:
Northeastern Siberia

ERA:
1000 CE

If underwear was so expensive, what did early parents do for their babies?

Around 1000 CE, some cultures used plants for diapers. The Chukchi in northeastern Siberia padded baby bottoms with reindeer moss under sealskin pants.

PHRRT

Plants were also the original disposable diaper. The Navajo in southwestern North America used shredded desert cliffrose for babies on cradleboards.

LOCATION:
Southwestern
North America

ERA: 1400 CE

Plants as pants?!
The original
"call of nature"!

PBPBPB
PHRRT

LOCATION:
England

ERA:
1300–1700 CE

Throughout history, underwear differed not only by region but also by age, class, and gender.

English knights in the thirteenth and fourteenth centuries wore full-bodied underwear to protect and pad against armor.

English kings around this time preferred clothing that showed off power and wealth. Henry VIII liked wearing fancy underwear on the outside called a codpiece. Cod here meaning *bag*. Not the fish.

Meanwhile, Henry's wives wore underwear on their heads! That's right—in the sixteenth century, fine ladies wore head underwear called a coif. The linen or silk coif was covered by a hat or hood while visiting friends or touring town.

During the European Renaissance, English ladies also wore boring old chemises. However, as years went by, ladies' underwear became bigger and

BIGGER.

1500–1550 CE
Simple chemise.

1650–1700 CE
Stays lengthen, chemises have more embellishments, and farthingales fall out of style.

1700–1750 CE
Farthingales make a comeback, this time with an oval shape.

1550–1600 CE
Spanish farthingale is added.

1600–1650 CE
A pair of bodies (later called stays or corsets) and the cartwheel farthingale become more common underwear.

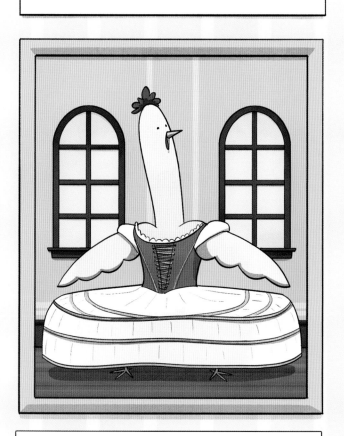

1750–1800 CE
Side hoops extend skirts even wider.

Oof. That hurts.

1800–1850 CE
Stays are renamed corsets—
from the French word for *body*.
Tight lacing becomes the trend.

In Asia, Chinese undergarments experienced similar shifts and lifts over time.

206 BCE–220 CE (Han dynasty)
Baofu and xinyi keep wearers'
bellies warm.

220–589 CE (Six Dynasties)
Liangdang is similar to the xinyi
but the back is covered.

**618–907 CE
(Tang dynasty)**

The strapless hezi lets wearers have open necklines and bare arms.

**960–1279 CE
(Song dynasty)**

Moxiong makes higher necklines the fashion again. Neckties and fabrics varied with wealth.

**1279–1368 CE
(Yuan dynasty)**

Hehuan jin features a strapless top similar to the hezi, with buttons in the front or a tie in the back.

1368–1644 CE (Ming dynasty)

Zhuyao covers less of the belly, with a tightness around the waist.

**1644–1911 CE
(Qing dynasty)**

Dudou has a neck strap, back strap, and upside-down triangle bottom.

LOCATION:
United States of America
ERA:
1800-1900 CE

Of course, every culture had those who marched to their own cluck. Some—like American Civil War surgeon Mary Walker—traded petticoats for pants so she could more easily serve in active battle. Despite Mary's earning the Presidential Medal of Honor, others couldn't look past her clothes.

The Chicken Times

Mary was arrested several times for impersonating a man, but she said, "I don't wear men's clothes. I wear my own clothes."

Mary wasn't the only one breaking free from tight corsets: An American revolution of underwear was underway.

1870s–1910s: Men and women wear "emancipation" underwear (union suits).

1920s: Men's union suits get shorter. Women wear step-in chemises.

1930s: Men's underwear debuts Y-front briefs. Bras and high-waist shorts become popular for women.

1960s: Spandex makes underwear stretchier for everyone.

1970s: Bright colors and bold patterns are popular. Thong underwear is invented.

1940s: Wartime simplicity: Some men drop the undershirt as part of their underwear. Nylons replace silk stockings for women.

1950s: Glamorous fashions return: undershirts, boxers, and sock suspenders for men. Women wear girdles and bullet bras.

1980s: Underwear waists move higher, as do women's leg openings.

1990s: Brand-name waistbands trend for both men and women.

2000s: Elastic girdles (like Spanx) become the modern corsets for fancy events.

Today's underwear is cheaper and comes in more styles than ever before, and with modern machines, making them is a snap.

Some underwear is still designed for special jobs.

Other types of underwear are made for specific ages.

And cultural tastes still matter.

Luckily, you get to pick the underwear that works for you.

Professor Chicken's Extra Credit

Although underwear is the butt of many jokes, it holds serious clues about life in the past. Think like a detective and unravel hints about how people lived then and now.

Under . . . where?

Ancient underwear can tell you about the places and spaces where people lived. For example, what animals did they have? Were these animals wild or domestic? Take Ötzi's loincloth. It was made of sheepskin.

What clues does that give you about Ötzi's life?

Underwear also gives clues about plant life. For example, skilled workers in Uganda used bark from the Mutaba tree to make clothing. In Tonga, material is similarly harvested from the paper of the mulberry tree. Both cultures made bark cloth, but each used raw materials from their natural environments.

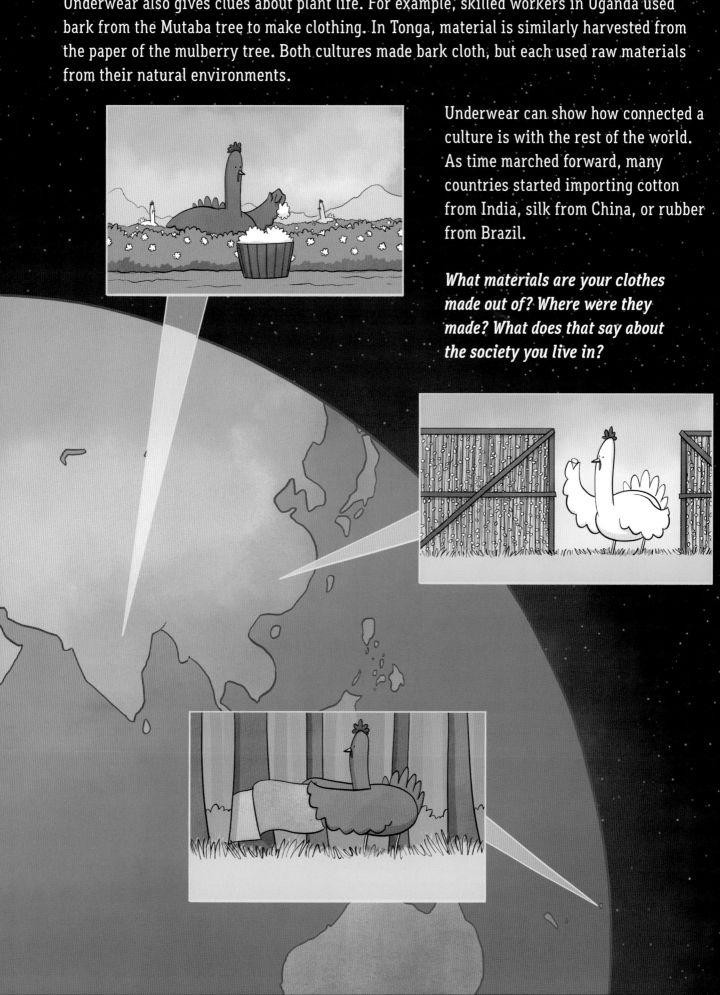

Underwear can show how connected a culture is with the rest of the world. As time marched forward, many countries started importing cotton from India, silk from China, or rubber from Brazil.

What materials are your clothes made out of? Where were they made? What does that say about the society you live in?

Under . . . what?

Underwear gives hints about a culture's technology. Does the corset have metal eyelets? That didn't become common until after the Industrial Revolution. Does the underclothing have temperature-control technology? That's thanks to research for the NASA space program.

A few additional inventions made underwear-making a snap:
- Water-powered cotton-spinning machines sped up the process of making thread. (1769 CE)
- Powered weaving looms accelerated cloth-making. (1785 CE)
- The sewing machine revolutionized making clothes. (1830 CE)
- Vulcanized rubber opened the door for elastic and other stretchy fabrics. (1839 CE)

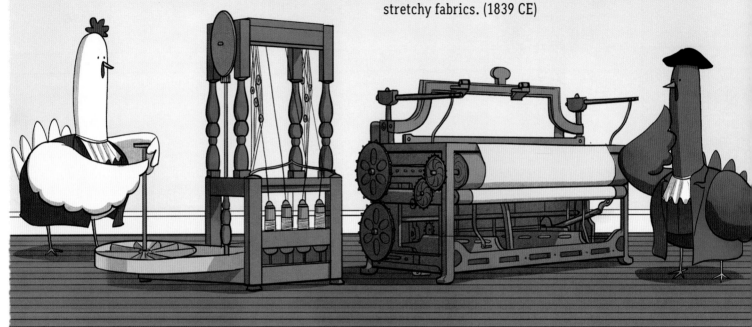

How was your clothing made? What machines were needed? Who helped make it?

Under . . . why?

Underwear can signal what a culture values. Some cultures, like Elizabethan England, valued a society where everyone knew their place, and that place was governed down to their underwear.

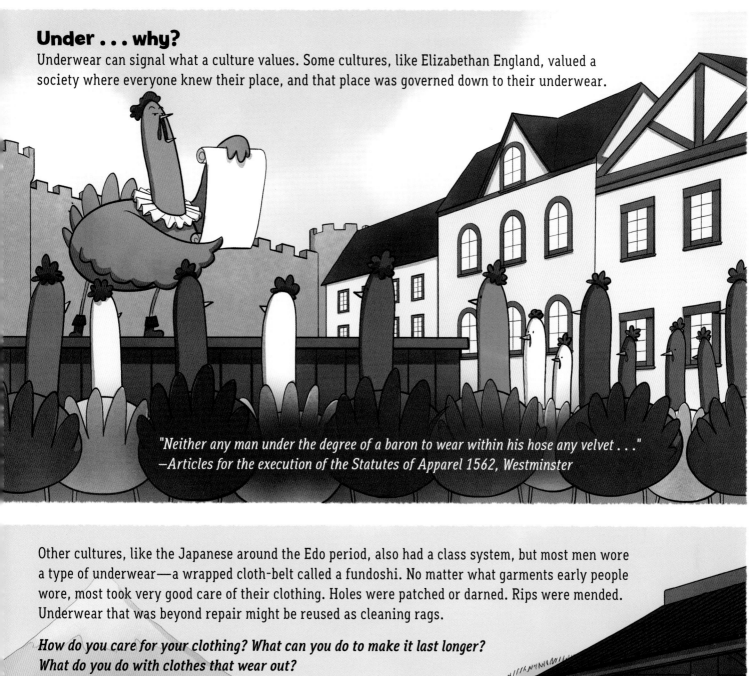

"Neither any man under the degree of a baron to wear within his hose any velvet . . ."
—Articles for the execution of the Statutes of Apparel 1562, Westminster

Other cultures, like the Japanese around the Edo period, also had a class system, but most men wore a type of underwear—a wrapped cloth-belt called a fundoshi. No matter what garments early people wore, most took very good care of their clothing. Holes were patched or darned. Rips were mended. Underwear that was beyond repair might be reused as cleaning rags.

How do you care for your clothing? What can you do to make it last longer?
What do you do with clothes that wear out?

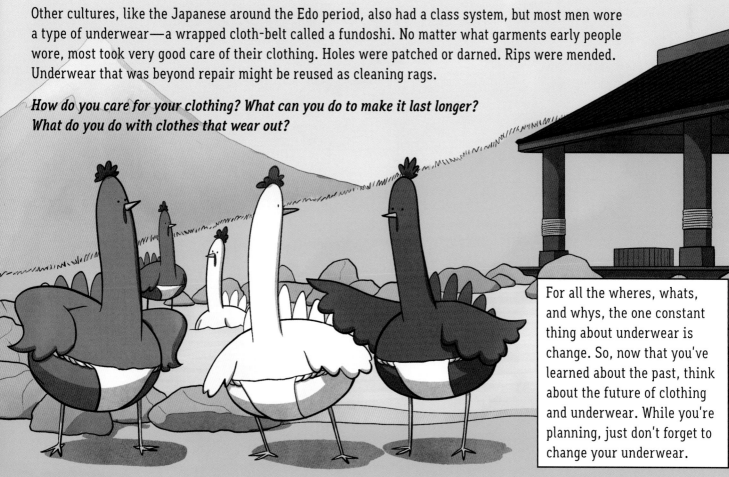

For all the wheres, whats, and whys, the one constant thing about underwear is change. So, now that you've learned about the past, think about the future of clothing and underwear. While you're planning, just don't forget to change your underwear.

~3000 BCE: Ötzi the Iceman rocks his leather loincloth.

~1325 BCE: King Tutankhamen is buried with linen loincloths.

~400 BCE: Roman women wrap their chests with a tight-fitting band.

~1470 CE: A large wooden underskirt called the farthingale is invented in Spain.

~1500 CE: English knights wore padded, full-bodied underwear.

~1600 CE: "A pair of bodies" are common underwear for English women.

~1850 CE: Hoop skirts are invented in Paris.

~1870 CE: Emancipation union underwear is invented in New York.

~1880 CE: Japanese men wear fundoshi.

1942 CE: Perma-Lift advertises a cone-shaped bra.

1959 CE: Spandex is used in underwear.

1974 CE: Rudi Gernreich invents the thong bikini.

~200 CE: Chinese women dress in boafu.

~1000 CE: Chukchi mothers pad baby bottoms with moss.

~1300 CE: Men in England wear baggy linen undershorts called linen braies.

~1710 CE: Panniers extend European skirts wider.

~1810 CE: Western women wear pantalets under skirts.

~1830 CE: Layers of stiff horsehair petticoats become common in Europe.

1913 CE: Mary Phelps Jacob obtains a patent for the modern bra.

1935 CE: Y-front briefs debut for men.

1939 CE: Nylon stockings appear at the World's Fair in New York.

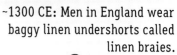

1990s: NASA develops temperature-control materials. Underwear companies adopt it.

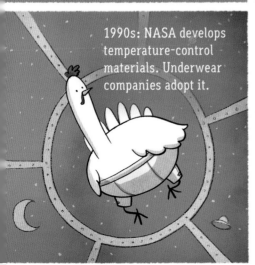

2007 CE: A British company launches underwear with a fart filter.

TOOT

PROFESSOR CHICKEN

Selected Bibliography

"A Brief History of Underwear." *A History of Underwear*. localhistories.org/underwear.html.

Cartwright, Mark. "Roman Gladiator." *Ancient History Encyclopedia*. Last modified May 3, 2018. ancient.eu/gladiator/.

Chisholm, James S. *Navajo Infancy: An Ethological Study of Child Development*. New Brunswick, NJ: Aldine Transaction, 2009.

"Corset Timeline." *History of Corsetry*. tahliamckellartextiles.weebly.com/corset-timeline.html.

Deng, Peng Ju. *Underwear Design*. Shenyang: Liaoning Science and Technology Press, 2009.

"Elizabethan Era Sumptuary Laws for Men and Women." *Elizabethan Era*. elizabethanenglandlife.com elizabethan-era-sumptuary-laws.html.

Ewing, Elizabeth. *Fashion in Underwear: From Babylon to Bikini Briefs*. Mineola, NY: Dover, 2010.

Feltman, Rachel. "What Was Otzi the Iceman Wearing When He Died? Pretty Much an Entire Zoo." *The Washington Post*. August 18, 2016. washingtonpost.com/news/speaking-of-science /wp/2016/08/18/what-was-otzi-the-iceman-wearing-when-he-died-pretty-much-an-entire -zoo/?noredirect=on&utm_term=.15ae1d23c7af.

Fowler, Brenda. "Forgotten Riches of King Tut: His Wardrobe." *The New York Times*. July 25, 1995. nytimes.com/1995/07/25/science/forgotten-riches-of-king-tut-his-wardrobe.html.

Keyser, Amber J. *Underneath It All: A History of Women's Underwear*. Twenty-First Century Books, 2018.

Killgrove, Kristina. "Caesar Undressing: Ancient Romans Wore Leather Panties And Loincloths." *Forbes*. June 19, 2015. forbes.com/sites/kristinakillgrove/2015/06/19/caesar-undressing-ancient -romans-wore-leather-panties-and-loincloths/#166181186.

Lineberry, Cate. "'I Wear My Own Clothes.'" *The New York Times*. December 2, 2013. opinionator.blogs.nytimes.com/2013/12/02/i-wear-my-own-clothes/.

"Meet Dr. Mary Walker: The Only Female Medal of Honor Recipient." *U.S. Army*. army.mil/article/183800 /meet_dr_mary_walker_the_only_female_medal_of_honor_recipient.

Monson, Marianne. *Women of the Blue & Gray: True Civil War Stories of Mothers, Medics, Soldiers, and Spies*. Shadow Mountain, 2018.